OBJECTIVE
KET

Annette Capel
Wendy Sharp

Workbook with Answers

CAMBRIDGE
UNIVERSITY PRESS

CAMBRIDGE UNIVERSITY PRESS
Cambridge, New York, Melbourne, Madrid, Cape Town,
Singapore, São Paulo, Delhi, Tokyo, Mexico City

Cambridge University Press
The Edinburgh Building, Cambridge CB2 8RU, UK

www.cambridge.org
Information on this title: www.cambridge.org/9780521619950

First published 2005
9th printing 2012

Printed in the United Kingdom at the University Press, Cambridge

A catalogue record for this publication is available from the British Library

ISBN 978-0-521-61995-0 Workbook with answers
ISBN 978-0-521-54149-7 Student's Book
ISBN 978-0-521-54150-3 Teacher's Book
ISBN 978-0-521-54151-0 Audio Cassettes (2)
ISBN 978-0-521-54152-7 Audio CDs (2)
ISBN 978-0-521-61994-3 Workbook
ISBN 978-0-521-74461-4 KET for Schools Practice Test Booklet with answers with Audio CD
ISBN 978-0-521-17897-6 KET for Schools Practice Test Booklet without answers
ISBN 978-0-521-74466-9 Student's Book Pack (Student's Book and KET for Schools
                     Practice Test Booklet without answers with Audio CD)

Cover design by Dale Tomlinson

Designed and produced by Kamae Design, Oxford

Contents

Grammar

1 Answer the questions in this chart about you and your friend. Then read the right description for you. Is it correct? Do you like the suggestions?

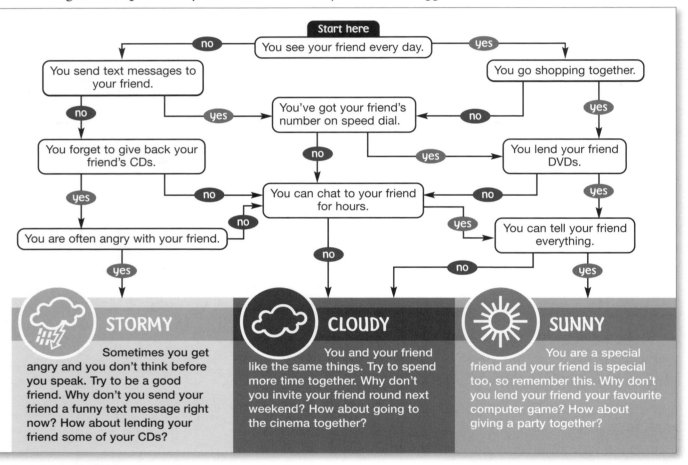

2 Make questions from the sentences in the chart.

EXAMPLE:

0 You send text messages to your friend.
Do you send text messages to your friend?

1 ....
2 ....
3 ....
4 ....
5 ....
6 ....
7 ....
8 ....

3 Now make *Wh-* questions or suggestions from these words.

EXAMPLE:

0 (brother your got your all why has CDs?)

Why has your brother got all your CDs?

1 (ice cream is favourite your what?)

....

2 (meet cinema me when you can the at?)

....

3 (about Laura party on how to inviting your Saturday?)

....

4 (tonight what you got for homework have?)

....

5 (don't DVD borrow from why Juan you the?)

....

6 (does girl long the with from hair where the come?)

....

Writing

4 Answer these questions. Write in sentences.

EXAMPLE:

0 How old are you? .... *I'm 12.* ....

1 How old is your best friend?

....

2 When do you go out together?

....

3 Where do you meet your friend?

....

4 What CDs has your friend got?

....

5 Who is your favourite film star?

....

Vocabulary

5 Find eleven more adjectives in this word square. Look → and ↓.

u	s	p	e	c	i	a	l	i
i	l	l	r	o	p	n	e	g
n	i	e	l	l	m	g	n	o
t	g	a	t	c	f	r	e	e
a	r	s	c	h	u	y	n	g
l	e	e	s	w	n	e	t	o
s	a	d	e	l	n	g	h	o
a	t	r	u	e	y	b	a	d
k	n	b	o	r	i	n	g	s

6 Use some of the adjectives to complete the meanings.

EXAMPLE:

0 The word ....*special*........ describes something or someone important.

1 Something that makes you laugh is
   ....

2 If something isn't a lie, it's ....

3 The word .... is the opposite of the word *happy*.

4 When you don't feel well, you are
   ....

5 The word .... describes something that is not interesting.

6 If you say a film is very ...., you really like it.

2 Shopping

Vocabulary

1 How do you learn new vocabulary? Write words in groups. Add nouns from Unit 2 to these lists.

Bookshop: *map*
Chemist: *aspirin*
Newsagent: *magazine*

2 The words below are all things you find in a department store but the letters are in the wrong order. Add the words to the correct floor in the department store. Start with the letter shown. Most of the words are plurals.

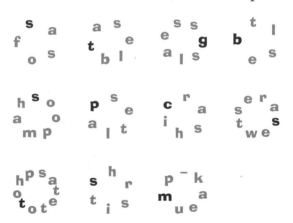

3 Complete the crossword. The number of letters is given in brackets.

Across
1 The plural of *child*. (8)
5 Windows are made of this. (5)
6 A large animal with four legs. (5)
7 A green or red fruit. (5)
8 You can find places or roads on this. (3)
9 These live in water and are good to eat. (4)
11 New shoes are put in these. (5)
12 The plural of *foot*. (4)

Down
2 Costs 50% less. (4, 5)
3 The plural of *dish*. (6)
4 Read this if you are interested in the news. (9)
10 A child can play with this. (3)

sofas

2

1

G

B

Grammar

4 Look at these two pictures of a market and find the differences. Use *some* or *any* to complete the sentences about picture B.

EXAMPLE:

0 They've got ...... *some onions* ....

1 They've got .... from Spain.
2 There are ....
3 There aren't ....
4 They .... apples.
5 They've got .... large .... but they haven't got .... small ones.
6 They haven't got .... left.

5 Choose the correct word, A, B or C.

EXAMPLE:

0 I'd like .... information about shopping online.
Ⓐ some   **B** an   **C** one

1 How .... chocolate did you eat?
A many   **B** much   **C** more

2 There's a great racing bike .... sale here.
A for   **B** in   **C** at

3 Can you get me .... sandwiches at the supermarket?
A any   **B** one   **C** some

4 Were there .... people at the party?
A much   **B** many   **C** most

5 I buy two computer magazines .... month.
A some   **B** each   **C** all

6 Did you spend your birthday money .... clothes?
A with   **B** of   **C** on

7 This book has .... very funny stories in it.
A some   **B** any   **C** a

8 There aren't .... green and white T-shirts left.
A more   **B** much   **C** many

Writing

6 Finish these sentences about shopping.

1 My favourite shop is ....
2 I go shopping with ....
3 I'd like to buy .... for my friend's birthday.
4 I don't spend ....
5 The supermarket near us sells cheap ....
6 You can buy .... on the internet.

3 Food and drink

Grammar

1 Write the correct sentence for each face.

EXAMPLES:

  0 ☺ He / like / ice cream.
    He likes ice cream.

00 ☹ He / eat / fish.
    He doesn't eat fish.

  1 ☹ I / like / chocolate.

  2 ☹ My friend / buy / apples.

  3 ☺ Marco / make / salad.

  4 ☺ Anna / love / cheese.

  5 ☹ The cat / drink / milk.

  6 ☹ We / grow / bananas.

  7 ☺ The cafe / sell / cola.

  8 ☹ My father / use / a cookbook.

  9 ☺ My grandmother / cook / our dinner.

10 ☹ Tessa and Piero / come / home for lunch.

2 Put the adverb of frequency (*never*, *usually*, etc.) in the correct place. One sentence is already correct.

EXAMPLE:

0 You eat never rice with a knife.
   You never eat rice with a knife.

1 We have dinner always at six thirty.

2 The food festival usually is in August.

3 Mauro has often a cake on his birthday.

4 My brother is late never for meals!

5 Do you drink coffee usually in the afternoon?

6 Sometimes I buy a sandwich for lunch.

7 I shop always at the supermarket.

8 My mother invites my friends often to dinner.

3 What's the time? Write sentences giving the time on the clock. Sometimes more than one answer is possible.

EXAMPLE:

0 *It's one ten. It's ten minutes past one.*

1	2	3	4	5	6

1 ....

2 ....

3 ....

4 ....

5 ....

6 ....

Vocabulary

4 The words below are all fruit and vegetables but some of the letters are missing. Add the missing vowels (*a, e, i, o, u*) to complete the words.

EXAMPLE:
0 rng   *orange* ....

1 crrt   ....
2 lmn   ....
3 ptt   ....
4 ppl   ....
5 tmt   ....
6 bnn   ....
7 grp   ....

Writing

5 Complete these sentences with true information about you.

1 My birthday is on ....
2 On my birthday I always ....
3 I never .... on my birthday.
4 At my party I ....
5 My friends sometimes ....

Exam skills

6

Reading Part 1

Which notice (**A–H**) says this (**1–5**)?

For questions **1–5**, choose the correct letter **A–H**.

Example:

0 It's a good idea to telephone first before you arrive.

Answer:

---

1 Pay less than usual at this restaurant.

2 You can get a meal here at any time.

3 You do not need to cook these.

4 You must pay for your meal in cash.

5 You can get a job here.

A   *Restaurant closed all weekend.*

B   If you want to eat here, you must book a table.

C   **Buy takeaway meals here!**

D   **Pizza House** – no cheques or credit cards please.

E   Waiter or waitress wanted to work evenings.

F   **Please pay the waitress.**

G   **Cafe open all day, every day.**

H   **This week** - *Free* drink with every meal.

4 The past

Grammar

1 Put the verbs in brackets in the past simple.

Ferdinand Magellan (1480–1521)

In 1519 Ferdinand Magellan (0) _left_ (leave) Spain. He (1) .... (take) five ships with him. He (2) .... (want) to find the East Indies. Unfortunately, the trip (3) .... (not start) well because there (4) .... (be) 60 days of rain. His ships first (5) .... (go) south towards Africa and then (6) .... (cross) the Atlantic Ocean. They then (7) .... (travel) past South America and there one ship was lost because there (8) .... (be) very high seas and stormy winds. The sailors on another ship (9) .... (decide) to go back to Spain but Magellan's ship (10) .... (not stop).

In the Pacific Ocean they sometimes (11) .... (not have) any wind and there (12) .... (not be) much food or water. After some time the ships (13) .... (arrive) in the Philippines. Here Magellan (14) .... (die), but after many problems one of his ships – the _Victoria_ – (15) .... (get) home safely to Spain. The _Victoria_ (16) .... (take) two years and 353 days to travel all around the world.

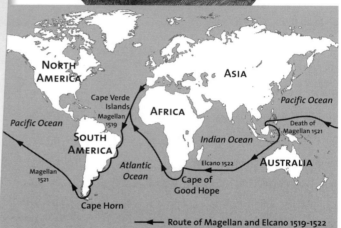

Route of Magellan and Elcano 1519-1522

1 ....
2 ....
3 ....
4 ....
5 ....
6 ....
7 ....
8 ....
9 ....
10 ....
11 ....
12 ....
13 ....
14 ....
15 ....
16 ....

2 Write questions and answers about Magellan's trip.

EXAMPLE:

0 Where / he / leave from?
   Where did he leave from ? He _left from Spain_ .

1 How / he / travel?
   ....? He ....

2 How many / ships / he / take?
   ....? He ....

3 Where / he / lose / a ship?
   ....? He ....

4 How much / food and water / they / have?
   ....? They ....

5 Where / Magellan / die?
   ....? Magellan ....

6 Which ship / get / home / safely?
   ....? The ....

7 How long / take / the _Victoria_ to travel around the world?
   ....? It ....

3 What are the past simple forms of these irregular verbs?

0 begin	*began*	8 pay	
1 catch		9 say	
2 choose		10 speak	
3 drink		11 stand	
4 fly		12 think	
5 grow		13 wear	
6 make		14 write	
7 meet		15 do	

Exam skills

4

Writing Part 6

Read the descriptions (**36–40**) of different transport.

What is the word for each one?
The first letter is already there. There is one space for each other letter in the word.

Example:

0 This will take you anywhere you want, if you pay.   t _ _ _

> *Answer:* | **0** | taxi |

---

36 You often travel in this on a school trip.
c _ _ _ _

37 Marco Polo travelled on one of these.
h _ _ _ _

38 It's fun to go in one of these on the river.
b _ _ _

39 People today like to travel on this to other countries.
p _ _ _ _

40 Children like to ride these.
b _ _ _ _ _ _ _

Writing

5 Sort the sentences below into two notes. Match what they say with the questions A and B. Re-write them on the emails.

> I went to see my cousin Sandro in New York.

> Last week I went to Thailand.

> My friend Jo came with me and we had a great time.

> I stayed in a big hotel near the beach.

> I went swimming and played tennis every day.

> We went by plane from Heathrow airport.

A You want to write an email to a friend about a trip you took.

Say:
• **when** you went
• **where** you stayed
• **what** you did.

B You want to write an email to a friend about a trip you took.

Say:
• **why** you went
• **who** you went with
• **how** you travelled.

A
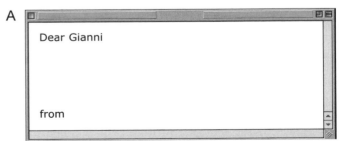

Dear Gianni

from

B

Dear Emilio

from

5 Animals

Vocabulary

1 Complete this animal crossword. The number of letters is given in brackets.

1 These pets eat mice and feel soft. (4)
2 You can swim in the sea with these animals. (8)
3 These animals live in Africa. (5)
4 People like to ride this animal. (5)
5 You can find these animals in South East Asia and Africa. (9)
6 This animal lives in rivers and the sea. (4)
7 Some of these animals live in the Arctic. (5)
8 This animal lives in the trees in hot countries. (6)
9 These animals have eight legs. (7)
10 This is a popular pet. (3)

2 Complete the sentences using the present simple or past simple of one of these verbs.

make   do   take   spend

EXAMPLE:

0 I (not) *didn't do* my homework last night because I took my dog for a walk.

1 Every morning I .... my own breakfast before going to college.
2 We .... the shopping for food for the animals yesterday.
3 Hugo .... some photos of his cat and dog playing.
4 Everyone .... the English exam last Friday morning.
5 I .... an appointment with the vet when my dog was ill.
6 How much money (you) .... at the zoo on Saturday?
7 I .... nothing at the weekend, just played with my pet spider.
8 Fabio .... a phone call to the aquarium to ask about opening times.
9 On holiday last year, we .... some time watching polar bears.
10 Susie .... some money over the holidays by feeding her friend's cat.

Grammar

3 Read the article and choose the correct word, A, B or C.

The Penguin

Penguins are a type of bird (0) ..*B*.. they are found in Antarctica, South America and South Africa. (1) .... are 17 different types of penguin (2) .... each kind lives in large groups. The largest penguin is the Emperor penguin.

Penguins are birds (3) .... they can't fly! They spend most of (4) .... time swimming. They eat fish (5) .... they can swim for hundreds of kilometres to look for food. Penguins sleep for a few minutes at a time, at any time of the day or night. They stand up (6) .... they sit down to sleep.

Penguins are black and white. These are good colours (7) .... they keep the penguins safe. (8) .... backs are dark like the sea and so when (9) .... swimming it's hard to see them from the air. The front of the penguin's body is white like the ice so no hungry animal can see it from under the water.

0 A or	B and	C but
1 A There	B Their	C They're
2 A and	B because	C but
3 A or	B because	C but
4 A their	B there	C they're
5 A because	B and	C or
6 A or	B but	C because
7 A but	B or	C because
8 A There	B They're	C Their
9 A they're	B there	C their

4 The sentences below are about goldfish. Join the sentences together using *and, or, but* or *because*. There can sometimes be more than one answer.

EXAMPLE:

0 I wanted a goldfish for my birthday. I really like them.
I wanted a goldfish for my birthday because I really like them.

1 Goldfish are easy to look after. They cost less to buy than a cat or a dog.

....

2 Goldfish can live in a glass bowl. It is important to change the water every week.

....

3 You can put different things in your goldfish bowl, like a small castle. You can grow plants in it.

....

4 Give your goldfish food two to three times a day. Give it only a small amount.

....

5 You can go on holiday. Don't forget to ask a friend to look after your goldfish.

....

Writing

5 Correct the spelling and linking words in this email to a friend.

Elisa
You can go to the zoo in our town to see beers, penguins, elefants. It is open every weekend because we can go toogether. We can travell by bus and go by car, if you want. I like the penguins best but they swim so wel underwater.
See you son.

Elisa
....
....
....
....
....

Leisure and hobbies

Vocabulary

1 Here are some spelling errors that candidates have made in the KET exam. Correct the sentences.

EXAMPLE:

0 I'd like to do something <u>diferent</u> today.

........*different*........

1 The new tenis court is beatiful.

....

2 My unkle and ant are coming to diner today.

....

3 Can you telefone me tomorow?

....

4 My appartement is on the segond floor.

....

5 My freinds are going to the cinama this afternoon.

....

6 This book is very intresting.

....

7 I think English is easyer than Japanese.

....

8 This ride is biger and beter than that one.

....

2 Look at the pictures and write the first letter of each word in the boxes below. These letters make the name of a sport. What is it?

3 Put these sentences from this telephone call in the correct order.

.... OK, see you then. Bye.

.... Oh, hi, Cecilia. Claudia's at the beach.

.... No, it's Amanda. Claudia isn't in.

.... Sure, no problem.

........*1*........ Hi, is that Claudia?

.... Yes, I'll be at the party this weekend.

.... Hi, Amanda, it's Cecilia here.

.... Could you ask her to ring me this evening?

.... Great. See you soon, I hope.

   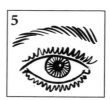

1	2	3	4	5	6	7	8	9	10	11
t										

Grammar

4 Put the adjectives in brackets in the comparative or superlative.

EXAMPLE:

0 The Aqua Park in my town is ..*the largest*.. (large) in the area.

1 Jonnie is .... (good) swimmer in my class.

2 He can swim .... (far) than anyone else.

3 Friday is .... (cheap) day to go to the Aqua Park.

4 My sister can go swimming for free because she is .... (young) than I am.

5 I bought a .... (expensive) swimming costume than my sister.

6 My sister swims .... (good) than I do.

7 I learnt to swim at an .... (early) age than she did.

8 The water in the swimming pool is .... (warm) than the sea.

9 The Aqua Park is .... (popular) place to go at the weekend.

10 The .... (late) the pool closes is 10.00 on a Saturday night.

Exam skills

5

Reading Part 2

Read the sentences about visiting a theme park.

Choose the best word (**A**, **B** or **C**) for each space for questions **6–10**.

Example:

0 Danny and Julia worked .... at school.

   A hard   **B** slow   **C** long

Answer:

---

6 So Danny and Julia .... their parents to take them to the theme park.

   A said   **B** asked   **C** spoke

7 They all .... to the theme park in the afternoon.

   A went   **B** visited   **C** moved

8 Danny and Julia were .... so their parents bought them a drink.

   A hungry   **B** tired   **C** thirsty

9 Danny wanted to try the .... ride.

   A fastest   **B** richest   **C** happiest

10 Danny and Julia .... all afternoon enjoying themselves.

   A spent   **B** did   **C** made

Writing

6 Correct the punctuation in this note to a friend.

> dear flavio last weekend i went to the city centre i went skateboarding with my best friend luca we had a great time there love pietro

Dear Flavio,

....

....

....

....

....

....

Clothes

Exam skills

1

Reading Part 5

Read the text about Serena Williams.

Choose the best word (**A**, **B** or **C**) for each space for questions **28–35**.

Serena Williams is a **(0)** .... popular tennis player. At the Australian Open tennis competition **(28)** .... January 2005, Serena Williams **(29)** ....   something special to Melbourne – her new fashion range. Serena helped to design **(30)** .... lime-green and white tennis clothes, which included an amazing dress and knee-high boots to go with **(31)** .... Serena showed these clothes to journalists in Melbourne. Under the dress, she **(32)** .... wearing a cutaway top and white shorts, which she later wore for all her matches.

The lime-green and white boots can be unzipped and taken off **(33)** .... the warm-up and the match. Serena said, 'My legs take a little **(34)** .... to warm up than most players, so they're perfect for me!'

Serena played very **(35)** .... in Melbourne and won the competition.

Example:

0 A very   **B** too   **C** so

Answer: 0

---

28 A on   **B** at   **C** in
29 A brings   **B** bringing   **C** brought
30 A a   **B** the   **C** one
31 A it   **B** them   **C** both
32 A is   **B** has   **C** was
33 A with   **B** between   **C** from
34 A long   **B** longer   **C** longest
35 A well   **B** good   **C** best

Grammar

2 Choose a verb for each space in the sentences. Remember to use the correct past tense.

ask   become   chat   look   make   ring
~~run~~   stop   throw   try on   wear

1 When my mobile phone (**a**) ....*rang*............ , I (**b**) .... a dress in a shop.

2 At the picnic, Sam (**a**) .... a new white dress. She (**b**) .... very angry when Harry (**c**) .... a large tomato at her. It (**d**) .... her dress and her face go really red!

3 Helen (**a**) .... to her friend Jo at the school gates when a man in a white ski jacket (**b**) .... past them. A few minutes later, a police car (**c**) .... and a policeman (**d**) .... Helen and Jo about the man – the police (**e**) .... for him.

3 Answer these questions using a continuous tense.

1 What were you wearing yesterday?

....

2 How many subjects were you studying two years ago?

....

3 What are you doing this evening?

....

4 Which football teams were playing last Sunday?

....

5 Who is coming to stay with you soon?

....

Vocabulary

4 Find thirteen more words to do with clothes in this word square. Look → and ↓.

s	j	a	s	o	c	k	s	t
i	a	l	w	o	o	l	h	r
z	c	b	e	l	t	g	i	o
e	k	h	a	t	t	r	r	u
e	e	x	t	h	o	s	t	s
s	t	e	e	w	n	h	w	e
s	h	o	r	t	s	o	h	r
a	t	r	a	i	n	e	r	s
r	t	b	u	t	t	o	n	r

Writing

5 Use some of the words from the word square in this description of the clown. Finish the final sentence in your own words.

Roger the Clown is wearing two different coloured (**0**) *socks* and a pair of short (**1**) .... His left (**2**) .... is much too big for him, but the right one is the correct (**3**) .... ! He is also wearing a (**4**) .... made of (**5**) .... with spots on and a very old (**6**) .... with only one (**7**) .... He has a (**8**) .... on his head – it looks really funny because (**9**) ....

Exam skills

1

Reading Part 1

Which notice (**A–H**) says this (**1–5**)?

For questions **1–5**, choose the correct letter **A–H**.

Example:

0 If you want to see the film, wait here.   *Answer:* 0 [A B **C**]

---

1 You can see a famous person at the theatre tonight.

2 Children cannot watch this film.

3 You could win a prize at this concert.

4 On one day a week, someone can see a play with you for nothing.

5 Some people may arrive late this evening because of the bad weather.

A Buy **one** theatre ticket and get **one free** – Mondays only

B *LATE-NIGHT FILMS EVERY FRIDAY*

C QUEUE FOR CINEMA TICKETS

D JOIN OUR FILM CLUB FOR LOWER PRICES & TALKS BY FAMOUS DIRECTORS

E *THIS EVENING'S PLAY STARS TOP TV ACTOR WARREN BLAKE*

F **SUMMER MUSIC FESTIVAL** Check your ticket number for tonight's competition

G CINEMA 2: *THE LIVING DEAD* – NOT FOR ANYONE UNDER 15

H TRAVEL PROBLEMS (SNOW) TONIGHT'S CONCERT WILL START AT 8.30 NOT 8.00

Grammar

2 Here are some errors that candidates have made in the KET exam. Correct the sentences.

EXAMPLE:

0 I may to see you next week. *I may see you next week.*

1 You can by train come here.
2 I can come in Monday or Friday.
3 Last night I must to do my homework.
4 You can go to the cinema IMAX.
5 I think that it may cost € 50.
6 I work in the week but you could came at the weekend.
7 You can feed the fishes at Mangabeiras Park.
8 I was at the back so I can't see anything.

3 Read each sentence and decide which modal verb is needed. Tick under *must*, *may* or *can't*.

EXAMPLE:

	must	may	can't
0 We / meet at the cinema no later than 8.00.	✓		

1 All actors / learn their words perfectly.
2 This story / be true – I don't believe it!
3 The actor / win an Oscar – I'm not sure.
4 I / remember any of the music from the film.
5 The film / have special effects – I don't know.
6 You / be 15 or older to see this film.

Vocabulary

4 The words below are all to do with music but the letters in the words are in the wrong order. Start with the letter shown. Write the words and match them to the descriptions 1–6.

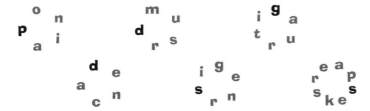

1 This is usually made of wood and has six strings.
2 People use these at concerts so that everyone can hear.
3 You do this by moving your feet.
4 The keys on this are black and white.
5 All rock bands need someone to play these.
6 This person uses their voice.

Exam skills

5

Writing Part 7

Complete this letter.

Write ONE word for each space for questions **41–50**.

Example: | **0** | for |

Dear Helen,

Thanks **(0)** .... your long letter from England. I really **(41)** .... music too! I saw Basement Jaxx last year when I went **(42)** .... a music festival here in Japan. **(43)** .... is called the Fuji Rock Festival. A man called Masahiro Hidaka started this festival. Nearly twenty years **(44)** .... he visited the Glastonbury Festival in your country and then decided to have **(45)** .... like that in Japan. The first festival in 1997 **(46)** .... in an amazing place – at the bottom of Mount Fuji – but now the festival is in Naeba Ski Resort, in Niigata. **(47)** .... are over 100,000 people at the festival **(48)** .... year. **(49)** .... don't you visit me in Japan next summer? We **(50)** .... go to the festival together!

Love, Tomoko

9 Travel

Grammar

1 These people are all making plans for their holidays. Decide which word or phrase best fits each space.

> I'm really excited (0) ...*because*... I'm going to America. We are going to (1) .... the Grand Canyon and visit Las Vegas. I think this holiday will definitely be the (2) .... holiday yet!

> On Tuesday I (3) .... fly to Canada to visit my aunt and uncle.

> (4) .... the holidays I plan to lie in the sun. I'm also going to have (5) .... fun with my friends.

> My family isn't going to go (6) .... this year, so I'm going to (7) .... as much time as possible with friends (8) .... are also at home. I'm going to play on my computer and (9) .... skateboarding.

  0 because/and
  1 watch/see
  2 better/best
  3 will / am going to
  4 In/On
  5 much / lots of
  6 anywhere/nowhere
  7 take/spend
  8 which/who
  9 play/go

2 Match a sentence in A with a sentence in B.

A
1 Ella is feeling really tired.
2 Pete wants to learn to ski.
3 The hotel room is too small and cold.
4 There's a sale on at the shops.
5 Tom has a new bike.
6 Anna likes fresh air.
7 I love dolphins.
8 I have a lot of friends.

B
a They're all going to get a postcard.
b She's going to go on a walking holiday.
c I'm going to Australia to swim with them.
d He's going to have some lessons.
e She's going to have a long holiday.
f Susie is going to buy some new summer clothes.
g I'm going to complain.
h He's going to go cycling this weekend.

3 Complete the sentences below about what you think will or won't happen to you in the future.

EXAMPLE:

0 marry   *I think I will marry a kind, good-looking person.*

1 money   ....

2 children   ....

3 job   ....

4 house   ....

5 holidays   ....

6 car   ....

7 be   ....

Vocabulary

4 Find nine more words in this word square from Unit 9. Look → and ↓.

e	a	s	j	o	u	r	n	e	y	y	s
a	u	s	i	e	a	a	s	w	r	h	w
r	w	o	r	r	b	o	o	k	d	n	i
t	c	u	t	u	s	i	i	r	l	k	t
h	c	v	r	s	p	a	c	e	m	n	z
o	f	e	a	f	t	k	u	q	c	x	e
l	l	n	v	b	y	l	e	u	a	s	r
h	y	i	e	x	c	r	u	i	s	e	l
y	v	r	l	c	i	f	r	y	g	z	a
w	d	s	t	n	f	c	s	f	m	w	n
a	g	a	u	s	t	r	a	l	i	a	d
q	h	s	k	b	d	v	b	d	t	k	h

Exam skills

5

Writing Part 6

Read the descriptions (**36–40**) of some things to do with holidays.
What is the word for each one?
The first letter is already there. There is one space for each other letter in the word.

Example:

0 You can sit here if you're by the sea.   b _ _ _ _

Answer: | **0** | beach |

---

36 You need a tent for this type of trip.   c _ _ _ _ _ _

37 You read this to choose a holiday.   b _ _ _ _ _ _ _

38 This is a good place to stay in.   h _ _ _ _

39 People who go on holiday.   t _ _ _ _ _ _ _

40 You can see interesting old objects here.   m _ _ _ _ _

Exam skills

1

Reading Part 4

Read the article about a family who live in a castle.

Are the sentences **21–27** 'Right' (**A**) or 'Wrong' (**B**)? If there is not enough information to answer 'Right' (**A**) or 'Wrong' (**B**), choose 'Doesn't say' (**C**).

I live in a castle!

Gabriel and his family moved from London to live in a castle in Scotland.

Our family decided that we all wanted to live together, so we looked in the newspapers and in 2002 my aunt and uncle found a castle we could buy. There are 17 of us altogether, including aunts, uncles and grandparents and we all have a room each. The castle is really big – it takes about ten minutes to walk from one side to the other.

It's really cold inside the castle, especially in winter. My aunt wears a coat inside as it's so cold. We only had one fire at first and there were no toilets when we moved in either! When I lived in London, the shops and school were very near. Here at the castle, it takes 20 minutes to get to the next village to go shopping. School is four kilometres away.

The best thing about living in the castle is that there is a lot of space – I can ride my bicycle all day in our large garden. I don't watch our television as much as I did. We now have electricity and bathrooms and a modern kitchen so things are much better than they were. I love living in a castle and I hope I can stay here forever!

Example:

0 Gabriel's aunt and uncle found a castle to buy on the internet.

---

21 There is enough space in the castle for the whole family.
   A Right   **B** Wrong   **C** Doesn't say

22 It's possible to get lost in the castle.
   A Right   **B** Wrong   **C** Doesn't say

23 There is no heating in the castle.
   A Right   **B** Wrong   **C** Doesn't say

24 Gabriel takes a bus to school.
   A Right   **B** Wrong   **C** Doesn't say

25 Gabriel enjoys being outside in the garden.
   A Right   **B** Wrong   **C** Doesn't say

26 There isn't a TV at the castle.
   A Right   **B** Wrong   **C** Doesn't say

27 Gabriel prefers to live in London.
   A Right   **B** Wrong   **C** Doesn't say

Vocabulary

2 Look at the pictures and write the first letter of each word below.
These letters make the names of two colours. What are they?
Do you know what colour these two colours make together?

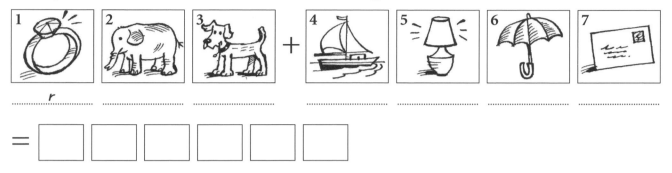

| 1 | 2 | 3 | + | 4 | 5 | 6 | 7 |

.......r......... ....

= ☐ ☐ ☐ ☐ ☐ ☐

Grammar

3 Look at the picture of a teenager's bedroom.
All these things weren't done yesterday. Use
these verbs to write sentences about what
wasn't done.

make ~~open~~ turn off ×2 clean
put in the wardrobe wash close

EXAMPLE:
0 Yesterday, the *curtains weren't opened.*

1 bed ....
2 room ....
3 clothes ....
4 cups and plates ....
5 TV ....
6 wardrobe door ....
7 light ....

4 Complete these sentences using a present simple passive or past simple passive
of the verb in brackets.

EXAMPLE:
0 The bridge across the river *is/was built* (build) of stone.

1 My room and my sister's room .... (paint) purple last year.
2 The Sagrada Familia .... (visit) by thousands of people every year.
3 Her old mobile .... (make) in Sweden.
4 For her birthday, my sister .... (give) a DVD player to go in her room.
5 Our garden .... (use) for parties in the summer.
6 Mauro's Ferrari .... (keep) locked in the garage.
7 Our apartment in New York .... (design) by a friend of my father's.

11 Sport

Vocabulary

1 Write the names of the sports in the photos.

a ......swimming......

b ....

c ....

d ....

e ....

2 Read the descriptions of words to do with these sports and write the name of each sport in each space.

EXAMPLE:

0 You use this to hit the ball in *table tennis* .

1 A person who goes .... stands up on this to ride the waves.

2 These are made of metal and help you to turn in the snow when you are ....

3 In .... , you can do this with your legs to move through the water more quickly.

4 You need to put this up on the sand to play beach ....

5 Your feet will hurt when you go .... if these aren't the right size for you!

6 Join this if you want to enter .... competitions at different pools.

7 This is the word for a group of people that plays against another group in sports like football and ....

8 If you want to go .... in the mountains, wear these on your hands.

9 As it says in its name, you play .... on this.

3 Now complete the word puzzle. What is the word for each description in Exercise 2? What is the sport in the grey box?

```
0           b  a  t
1        b  _  _  _
2  p  _  _  _  _
3           k  _  _  _
4        n  _  _
5     b  _  _  _  _
6     c  _  _  _  _
7     t  _  _  _
8        g  _  _  _  _  _
9     t  _  _  _  _
```

Grammar

4 Write questions for these answers.

EXAMPLE:

0 Snowboarding is easier than skiing and the clothes look great!
What _do you like_ about _snowboarding_ ?

1 I'm getting to Saturday's competition by car.
How .... ?

2 Christian Ronaldo plays football for Portugal.
Which .... ?

3 Gianni plays tennis with friends from his college.
Who .... ?

4 The gym is open until 10 pm.
When .... ?

5 The lights went out so the referee stopped the match.
Why .... ?

6 There were over 40,000 people in the stadium.
How .... ?

7 I'm going to go sailing on Lake Bolsena.
Where .... ?

5 **Complete the text with -*ing* forms of the verbs below. Use each verb once only.**

climb   cycle   dance   drive   exercise
keep   run   sit   ~~take~~

Holly loves (**0**) ....._taking_..... exercise and
(**1**) .... fit. Every morning before
breakfast, she goes (**2**) .... on her
bike. She hates (**3**) .... her car so she
usually walks to her office. Holly spends most
of her working day (**4**) .... at her
desk. Because of this, she puts on a T-shirt,
shorts and trainers at lunch time and goes
(**5**) .... in the park near her office.
When she gets back to work, she never
takes the lift and says she doesn't mind
(**6**) .... the stairs. After work, she
enjoys (**7**) .... for an hour at her
gym. On Tuesdays and Thursdays, she also
does samba (**8**) .... with friends
from work.

Exam skills

6

Reading Part 3

Complete the five conversations.

Choose **A**, **B** or **C** for questions **11–15**.

Example:

0

I can't come snowboarding with you because my leg hurts.

A What a pity!
B Why can't you?
C That's great!

Answer: **0** | A ■ | B □ | C □

---

11 Can you book a tennis court for next Wednesday?
A Which day shall we play?
B What time do you want to play?
C What sports can you play?

12 Why not play football with us this evening?
A You've got enough strikers!
B The stadium opens at 7.00.
C I usually win all my races.

13 I really hate going fishing!
A I didn't catch anything.
B I agree, it's so boring.
C I feel like doing that as well.

14 Snowboarding's more fun than skiing.
A How are your new skis?
B Where is it?
C Why do you say that?

15 Who's playing in goal today?
A Their new Norwegian keeper.
B There are three at the back.
C They're a very good idea.

12 The family

Vocabulary

1 The words in this exercise are all words for people in a family. Start with the letter shown and write the words.

1 ....
2 ....
3 ....
4 ....
5 ....
6 ....

Grammar

2 Circle the correct word.

EXAMPLE:

0 I saw Mr and Mrs Jones in the park with *their/theirs* grandson.

1 *Our/Ours* family isn't very big.
2 *Your/Yours* cousin is younger than *my/mine*.
3 Claudia's coming tonight. Let's meet outside *her/hers* flat at 7.00.
4 Dave and Jane's car is faster, so why don't we go in *their/theirs*?
5 Would you like to visit *my/mine* grandfather with me?
6 Can I have the address of that American cousin of *your/yours*?

Writing

3 Read the two postcards below and sentences 1–5. Which sentences answer questions in postcard A and which answer questions in postcard B?

A

Who came to your uncle's party? What was the food like? How did your uncle enjoy the party? Write to me soon! Best wishes, Ernesto

B

When did you last have a special meal with lots of your family? Why were you together? Did you enjoy yourself? Send me a postcard about it! Love, Yasmin

EXAMPLE:

0 I had a really great time! *B*

1 We were all there to see my cousin's new baby.
2 There was a lovely cake with 60 candles on it.
3 He really loved having us all together and he never stopped smiling!
4 Two weeks ago, my aunt invited us to her house in the country.
5 Everyone was there for Uncle Charles's birthday, including his brother from Australia.

4 Now write the sentences on the correct postcard below, A or B.
   Then finish each postcard.

Exam skills

5

Reading Part 5

Read the text about Giorgio Angelozzi.

Choose the best word (**A**, **B** or **C**) for each space for questions **28–35**.

Italian 'granddad' finds a family

At the age **(0)** .... 80, Giorgio Angelozzi felt sad because he **(28)** .... living alone. He decided to advertise for a 'new' family, and got letters from **(29)** .... , including Colombia!

Mr Angelozzi **(30)** .... a family in Bergamo in northern Italy. Elio and Marlena Riva answered the advert because Mr Riva's parents are dead and **(31)** .... parents live far away in Poland. Their children

Mateush, 18, and Dagmara, 16, are pleased to have a new grandfather because they miss **(32)** .... The teenagers, **(33)** .... both like loud music, say that they will be quieter at home now. Dagmara said: 'I just want to have a granddad. The rest is not important.'

In Italy today a lot of old people live by **(34)** .... , but perhaps Mr Angelozzi has started **(35)** .... new!

Example:

0	**A** of	**B** by	**C** in	*Answer:*	0	A ■ B ☐ C ☐

28	**A** is	**B** was	**C** has
29	**A** nowhere	**B** somewhere	**C** everywhere
30	**A** chose	**B** chooses	**C** chosen
31	**A** his	**B** her	**C** its
32	**A** ours	**B** yours	**C** theirs
33	**A** which	**B** who	**C** why
34	**A** yourselves	**B** ourselves	**C** themselves
35	**A** something	**B** anything	**C** nothing

13 The weather

Exam skills

1

Writing Part 7

Complete this letter.

Write ONE word for each space for questions **41–50**.

Example: | **0** | *a* |

> Dear Mario,
>
> Last week we had **(0)** .... big snowstorm.
> When I woke up two days **(41)** .... I looked
> out of my bedroom window **(42)** .... saw
> that everything was white. I went downstairs
> to listen **(43)** .... the radio. At eight
> o'clock they said that all the schools
> **(44)** .... closed and we could stay
> **(45)** .... home.
>
> I phoned my friends and we met in the park.
> There was a **(46)** .... of snow and so we
> had snowball fights. **(47)** .... I got home I
> was very wet and very tired. I **(48)** .... a
> hot bath and then **(49)** .... the evening
> watching TV.
>
> **(50)** .... you have any snow last week?
>
> Love,
> Luisa

Grammar

2 Write a sentence about questions 1–10 below
using *not as* .... *as*, *the same as* or an
adjective + *than*.

EXAMPLE:

0 Moscow cold −15° / New York cold −6°
Moscow is colder than New York. ....

1 Rome sunny 36° / Athens sunny 40°
....

2 Russia 17 million square kilometres /
Canada 9,971,000 square kilometres
....

3 River Nile 6,695 kilometres / river Amazon
6,516 kilometres
....

4 Eiffel Tower 300 metres / Empire State
Building 449 metres
....

5 Today cold / Yesterday cold
....

6 June ten hours sunshine / October six
hours sunshine
....

7 December no rain / January no rain
....

8 New Zealand / Antarctica
....

9 Venice / Rome
....

10 Mount Everest / Mount Kilimanjaro
....

3 Write sentences with *too* or *enough* and the adjectives below.

old
noisy
difficult
young
clean
small
ill
thin
hot
busy
~~cold~~

EXAMPLE:

0 It's too ....*cold*........ to go to school today.

1 I can't ski very well because I find it's too
....

2 My friend was feeling too .... to
go skating with me today.

3 The dog wasn't .... enough to go
through the small hole in the wall.

4 Peta's mother was too .... at
work to take her to the cinema.

5 Stefano was only nine and too
.... to see the film.

6 The teacher told me it wasn't ....
enough to open the outdoor swimming
pool.

7 Our street is very busy – sometimes it's too
.... to get to sleep.

8 Marco played in the snow yesterday and
today his shoes aren't .... enough
to wear to school.

9 The boy was too .... to reach the
high shelf.

10 The roof is too .... to stop the
rain coming inside.

Vocabulary

4 Put the weather words into the puzzle.
The last letter of each word is the first letter
of the next word.

thunderstorms
wind
snow
dry

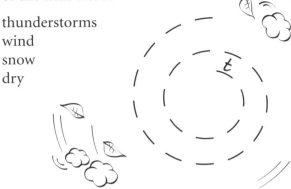

5 Complete the word puzzle with words about
the weather. What is the weather word in the
grey box?

0	s t o r m y
1	h _ t
2	w _ _ m
3	s _ _ _ y
4	r _ _ n
5	w _ _ _ y
6	c _ _ d

Writing

6 Correct the punctuation in this email to a
friend.

hi
in july the weather is quite good in my country it
doesnt rain very much so you dont need an
umbrella or a raincoat its better to bring tshirts
and a swimming costume when you come to visit
me dont forget a towel

Books and studying

Vocabulary

1 Can you find ten more words about books and writing in this circle?

word
dictionary
pen
terrible   park
artist
sentence   page   business
email   envelope
tourist   homework
building
journalist
parent
tape recorder   message
morning   occupation
note

2 Find seven more school subjects in this word square. Look → and ↓.

l	a	n	g	u	a	g	e	s	a	l
j	g	e	s	e	y	e	g	m	s	v
k	n	e	p	c	v	o	u	a	h	m
r	z	u	o	a	t	g	f	t	s	n
s	s	w	r	g	v	r	n	h	m	h
c	a	c	t	y	r	a	t	s	h	a
i	w	w	d	t	f	p	g	h	j	r
e	s	f	g	c	m	h	p	x	b	t
n	j	e	f	j	l	y	i	h	y	h
c	d	t	h	i	s	t	o	r	y	b
e	l	m	u	s	i	c	e	u	c	f

Exam skills

3

Reading Part 2

Read the sentences about going to a bookshop.

Choose the best word (**A**, **B** or **C**) for each space for questions **6–10**.

Example:

0 Jenny .... to spend some of her birthday money on a book.
A decided   **B** enjoyed   **C** thought

Answer: **0**   A■ B☐ C☐

---

6 On Saturday morning she .... a bus into town.
A went   **B** travelled   **C** took

7 She went into the bookshop and looked at the books on the ....
A cupboards **B** shelves   **C** desks

8 Jenny .... nearly an hour in the bookshop.
A spent   **B** left   **C** rested

9 She .... a book about Harry Potter.
A asked   **B** chose   **C** looked

10 The book was very .... – it had over 500 pages!
A high   **B** great   **C** heavy

Grammar

4 **Put these words in the correct order.**

EXAMPLE:

0 a white wooden large bookshelf
   a large white wooden bookshelf

1 a new nice comic

2 the old boring book history

3 a little lovely bookshop

4 the American expensive magazine

5 a French young famous writer

6 a university modern large library

7 the old dirty bookshelves

8 the English young friendly teacher

9 a little yellow lovely table

10 the Japanese excellent computers

5 **Complete these sentences with true information about you.**

EXAMPLE:

0 book / newspaper
   I prefer to read a book rather than a newspaper.

1 science fiction books / detective books

2 history / English

3 TV / study

4 the beach / a swimming pool

5 computer games / piano

Writing

6 **Read this note and correct the errors. There are ten more errors.**

Dear Elena,

Do you like reading? I do and ~~too~~ of my friends like it two. But sometimes their to many thinks to do and I don't have time too read.
Do you by a lot of books? I don't.
I use the library.
When I leave school I don't know weather I won't too teach or write books. What about you?

Buy for now!
Love,
Marisa

EXAMPLE:

0 _____ *two* _____

1 ....

2 ....

3 ....

4 ....

5 ....

6 ....

7 ....

8 ....

9 ....

10 ....

15 The world of work

Vocabulary

1 Read the descriptions and complete the jobs
   alphabet. The number of letters is shown.

a _ _ _ _   works in a theatre

bodyguard

c _ _ _   another word for a cook

d _ _ _ _ _   looks after your health

e _ _ _ _ _ _ _   makes or repairs machines

f _ _ _ _ _   works outside with animals

g _ _ _ _ _ _ _   looks after plants and flowers

h _ _ _ _ _ _ _ _ _   cuts your hair

i _ _ _ _ _ _ _ _ _   teaches you something – how to drive or ski, for example

j _ _ _ _ _ _ _ _ _   works on a newspaper

k _ _ _   the most important person in some countries

lifeguard

m _ _ _ _ _ _ _   works on cars and motorbikes

n _ _ _ _   looks after people in hospital

o _ _ _ _ _ _   a policeman, for example

p _ _ _ _ _ _ _ _ _ _ _   takes pictures

queen

r _ _ _ _ _ _ _ _ _ _   welcomes people in a hotel or office building

s _ _ _ a _ _ _ _ _ _ _ _   helps customers in a department store

t _ _ _ g _ _ _ _   takes a group of visitors sightseeing

undercover agent

v _ _ d _ _ _ _ _   drives something bigger than a car

w _ _ _ _ _   brings restaurant customers their food

xylophone player

yoga teacher

z _ _ _ _ _ _ _ _   like Paul in Unit 5

Grammar

2 Put the words in the correct order to make sentences using the past simple or present perfect. The time words show you which tense to use.

EXAMPLE:

0 Peppino / at the radio station / in 1977 / start / working

Peppino *started working at the radio station in 1977.*

1 Jan / the band's manager / since February / be

Jan ....

2 Helen / a pilot / become / three years ago

Three years ago, ...

3 Our class / yesterday / an artist's studio / visit

Our class ....

4 The Queen / give / Ellen MacArthur / after her round-the-world race / a special award in 2005

The Queen ....

5 Ben / before / study / chemistry / never

Ben ....

Exam skills

3

Reading Part 3

Complete the conversation between two friends. What does James say to Maria?
For questions **16–20**, mark the correct letter **A–H**.

Example:

Maria: Have you started working at the supermarket yet, James?

James: **0** ....

Answer: | 0 | A B C D E F G H |

Maria: How many hours a week are you doing?

James: **16** ....

Maria: You must feel tired on Thursdays!

James: **17** ....

Maria: I can understand that. Have you earned much money so far?

James: **18** ....

Maria: That's great! I'd like to get a job but my parents don't want me to.

James: **19** ....

Maria: I'll talk to them again tonight. Can you ask if the supermarket has any more jobs?

James: **20** ....

Maria: Thanks, James.

A Mine were the same, but they agreed in the end.

B They haven't paid me anything yet.

C It's okay usually, but sometimes I don't want to get up.

D Sure! I'll do that for you tomorrow.

E I work all day Saturday and on Wednesday evenings.

F They pay more on Sundays but I have to do college work then.

G Quite a lot. I've spent most of it on surfing clothes!

H I've been there for more than a month now.

Vocabulary

1 **Find sixteen more nouns and verbs to do with transport and travel in this word square. Two of them are two-word verbs. Look → and ↓.**

h	e	l	i	c	o	p	t	e	r
o	p	a	s	s	e	n	g	e	r
r	t	a	k	e	o	f	f	n	c
s	r	t	a	r	i	o	f	g	o
e	i	b	i	c	y	c	l	e	a
g	p	a	r	k	v	n	i	t	c
f	l	y	p	n	i	b	g	o	h
e	r	b	o	a	t	o	h	f	b
b	o	a	r	d	o	o	t	f	l
s	u	w	t	i	c	k	e	t	n

2 **Now match some of the words to these descriptions.**

EXAMPLE:

0 This person travels on a train, bus or other kind of transport. *passenger*

1 When you go through the gate and get on your plane, you do this.

2 This is a comfortable bus that is used for long journeys.

3 Planes leave from and arrive at this place.

4 This is another word for *journey*.

5 If you pay to put your car in a space, you do this.

6 Most airlines ask you to give them this with your passport when you check in.

7 You do this when the bus you are on has arrived at your stop.

Grammar

3 **Choose the correct modal verb in these sentences.**

EXAMPLE:

0 You *needn't/mustn't* get a ticket because you can buy one on the train.

1 You *should/need* catch the number 14 bus from the station.

2 We *can't/needn't* turn left here, so take the next one by the library.

3 FlyQuick customers *don't have to / must* check in at desk 51.

4 Drivers *mustn't/couldn't* park here until 6.30 p.m. tonight.

5 I think we *need/must* to get a taxi – it's too far to walk!

6 It *may/can* be possible to catch an earlier train – let me check.

7 You *need/don't have to* have the correct money as this machine gives change.

8 I *could/should* check the back wheel of your bike for you now if you want.

Writing

4 Correct the spelling errors in this postcard. There are nine more errors.

EXAMPLE:

0 ....*directions*....

1 ....
2 ....
3 ....
4 ....
5 ....
6 ....
7 ....
8 ....
9 ....

Dear Roz and Tim,
Here are some ~~direktions~~ to our house for next weekend. When you live the motorway, turn right at the rundabout – it'll say univirsity and city centre. Keep on that road for about two kilometres untill you come to a big petrol station whit a blue and yellow sign. Turn right their and go over the bridge. Just after you've crossed the river, you'll see the hospetal on your left. Take the second turning on the left after that – it's called Musium Street. We're at nummer 54.
See you on Saturday,
Love,
Sharon and Eduardo

Exam skills

5

Writing Part 8

Read the advertisement and the note.
Fill in the website form for questions **51–55**.

LONDON TO MADRID

Cheap one-way tickets
- from Luton airport, daily (21.20 arriving 00.15)
- from Heathrow airport – not Sats (05.40 arriving 09.10)

Luton   £31 (students £28.50)
Heathrow £52 (students £44.99 Mon & Tues only)

Visit our website now! www.adotravel.com

Hi Sam,
Here's the advert about flights, for our journey in April. Can you check their website for Tuesday 16th (morning flight)? As we're at college, it'll be under £45 each.
Thanks, Helen

ADOTRAVEL: WEBSITE FORM

Number of passengers:	**0** 2	Airport:	**53**
Travelling to:	**51**	Flight time:	**54**
Flight date:	**52**	Price per person:	**55**

CHECK FLIGHTS

17 Science and technology

Exam skills

1

Reading Part 5

Read the article about robots.

Choose the best word (**A**, **B** or **C**) for each space for questions **28–35**.

Robots

Most robots you see **(0)** .... films look a bit like people. They can walk and talk and, like people, can think about **(28)** .... best to do things. For example, some of the robots from the *Star Wars* films can speak **(29)** .... languages.

In real life, most robots work in factories **(30)** .... cars, but they don't look like **(31)** .... at all. The most common type of robot has one arm and no legs, and **(32)** .... just one job. Robots that are used in industry are controlled **(33)** .... computers. **(34)** .... robots never get bored. They can do the same work all day, every day. Let's hope that soon scientists **(35)** .... build robots to clean our houses!

Example:

0 **A** in   **B** on   **C** at

Answer: **0**

28 A what	**B** how	**C** which
29 A much	**B** many	**C** lot
30 A making	**B** made	**C** make
31 A we	**B** ours	**C** us
32 A does	**B** do	**C** did
33 A by	**B** for	**C** over
34 A They	**B** These	**C** This
35 A have	**B** must	**C** will

Grammar

2 Write sentences about why you do these things.

EXAMPLE:

0 have a shower
I have a shower to get clean.

1 phone my friends

2 listen to music

3 work hard at school

4 buy new clothes

5 use a computer

3 Here are some errors that KET candidates have made. Correct the sentences.

EXAMPLE:

0 Laura can to play tennis really well. *Laura can play tennis really well.*

1 Take the bus for getting to the town centre.
2 The best way for get back from the cinema is to take a taxi.
3 Go to classes for to learn computing.
4 We can go buying a new computer in the mall.
5 I am really happy you will come visit me.
6 It is better for you not play computer games.
7 It's a great place for take vacations.
8 I want get a new mobile.
9 You must to see that new film.
10 They decided buy a pink iPod mini.

Vocabulary

4 Use the words below in an appropriate form to complete the sentences. There may be more than one possible answer.

get   make   watch   see   take   do

EXAMPLE:

0 I'm going to ....*make*........ a cake tonight.

1 Last night I .... an old James Bond film on TV.
2 Don't hurry – you must .... your time.
3 Please don't .... any noise when you come home tonight.
4 I'm .... a guitar exam next week.
5 Susie is hoping to .... a job as a science teacher.
6 How much homework do you have to .... tonight?
7 Jonnie found it very difficult to .... friends at his new school.
8 My dad .... a lot of money painting houses.
9 My parents don't let me .... my friends in the evenings.
10 The girls went to the cinema to .... Brad Pitt in his new film.

5 The words below are all words about technology from Unit 17 but the letters are in the wrong order. Start with the letter shown and write the words.

1

t m r
c o
h o
a

....

2

e g o c
n h
t o
y o

....

3

e i n
e r
t t n

....

4

o v
e i
d

....

5

d t a
g e
g s
g

....

6

o o
b r
t

....

7

p p t
o l
a

....

8

s s a m
t g
t e
x e

....

Writing

6 Write an email to a friend about a computer game.

Say:
- **what** it is called
- **when** you got it
- **why** you like it.

Write **25–35** words.

18 Health and well-being

Exam skills

1

Reading Part 4

Read the article about sleep.

Are the sentences **21–27** 'Right' (**A**) or 'Wrong' (**B**)? If there is not enough information to answer 'Right' (**A**) or 'Wrong' (**B**), choose 'Doesn't say' (**C**).

Getting to sleep

Sleep is very important – in fact, it's just as important for your body as eating and exercising. If you don't get enough sleep, then you won't be able to enjoy yourself. Playing with friends, going swimming or even watching videos will not be much fun if you're tired.

People of all ages need sleep, but different people need different amounts. Babies sleep about twice as long as they stay awake. Teenagers need about eight or ten hours a night and older people need less – six

or seven hours. But one person may need more than another even if they are both the same age.

Six out of ten children say they are tired during the day, which means they are not getting enough sleep. So how can you get to sleep? A good idea is to write down what you are thinking about before you go to bed. Then, make sure your bedroom is as dark as possible and it isn't too hot or too cold. You can also try counting from 1 to 100 with your eyes closed. Don't drink cola before going to bed and don't do any sport in the evening. Reading an exciting book or watching an adventure film isn't a good idea either!

Example:

0 Sleeping is more important than eating.

0	A	B	C

---

21 If you're tired, you shouldn't go swimming.
   A Right   **B** Wrong   **C** Doesn't say

22 Babies spend more time sleeping than being awake.
   A Right   **B** Wrong   **C** Doesn't say

23 Not all adults need the same amount of sleep.
   A Right   **B** Wrong   **C** Doesn't say

24 It helps to keep your light on during the night.
   A Right   **B** Wrong   **C** Doesn't say

25 Remember to turn the heating off in your bedroom before you go to bed.
   A Right   **B** Wrong   **C** Doesn't say

26 You should do some exercise before going to bed.
   A Right   **B** Wrong   **C** Doesn't say

27 Avoid reading stories which will keep you awake.
   A Right   **B** Wrong   **C** Doesn't say

Vocabulary

2 **Which word is different? Why?**

EXAMPLE:

0 eye   ear   nose   foot
foot – not on your head

1 hand   arm   back   finger

2 police officer   doctor   chemist   nurse

3 truck   car   hospital   ambulance

4 a cold   a headache   a diet   a toothache

5 arm   leg   eye   neck

Grammar

3 **Put these words in the correct order.**

EXAMPLE:

0 friend my doctor to the this went morning see
My friend went to see the doctor this morning. OR This morning my friend went to see the doctor.

1 last had I throat a night sore

2 two a hospital ago very famous stayed I in weeks

3 very I like much doctor my

4 was I night sick the in

5 new my amazing is diet

6 need go I to chemist's the to today

7 take why aspirin you an don't?

8 this felt I afternoon terrible so home went I

4 **Put the verbs into the present simple and the future to make sentences in the first conditional.**

EXAMPLE:

0 If you _don't go_ (not go) to bed early, you _will fall asleep_ (fall asleep) in class.

1 If you .... (sleep) well, you .... (feel) well.

2 If I .... (go) to bed early, I .... (not get) to sleep for hours.

3 If you .... (eat) healthy food, you .... (live) longer.

4 If you .... (not eat) too many burgers and chips, you .... (stay) healthy.

5 You .... (earn) lots of money if you .... (become) a doctor.

6 What you .... (do) if you .... (get) a cold?

Writing

5 **Write a note to a friend about a dream you had.**

Say:
- **when** you had the dream
- **what** it was about
- **how** you felt when you woke up.

Write **25–35** words.

Language and communication

Grammar

1 Here are some errors that KET candidates have made with prepositions. Underline the errors and correct the sentences. One sentence is correct.

EXAMPLE:

0 I'm <u>in</u> holiday in Italy for two weeks. ....*on*.........

1 You can stay with my house. ....
2 I hope to meet you on the *Grand Hotel* at 10 a.m. ....
3 I don't mind sleeping in the floor. ....
4 I'll pick you up in the station. ....
5 It is the best beach of São Paulo. ....
6 Last night I was at a big party. ....
7 I have a new house at Paris, near the metro. ....
8 We will meet on the shopping centre. ....
9 I had dinner to a Yemeni restaurant. ....
10 You can visit the big museum at the city centre. ....
11 After a quarter of an hour, you'll arrive to Naples. ....
12 Now I live in 46 Federico Bardi Street. ....
13 We can meet on Perivale underground station at 11.30. ....

2 Complete the text about Norway with the correct prepositions of time.

(0) .....*In*..... 1814, Norway and Sweden became one country, but the Norwegian people weren't happy about this. There were many problems and finally, (1) .... May 17 1814, a new constitution was agreed, which was much better for Norway.

Then (2) .... the 1890s, there were more problems. (3) .... the beginning of the 20th century, it was clear that the two countries could no longer stay together. (4) .... the winter of 1904–05, many famous people talked of independence for Norway. The Norwegian explorer Fridtjof Nansen wrote a number of articles about this. (5) .... March 25 1905, one of his articles was printed in the British *Times* newspaper. Important French and German newspapers printed it too.

(6) .... June 1905, the Norwegian parliament said that Norway was no longer part of Sweden. The Swedes were angry but didn't want a war. They agreed to ask the Norwegian people to decide their future. (7) .... August 13 1905, 368,208 Norwegians voted for the separation and only 184 against. Women couldn't vote but about 250,000 of them signed a piece of paper to say 'yes' to the separation.

(8) .... the end of October 1905, Norway became an independent nation.

NORWAY

SWEDEN

Fridtjof Nansen

Vocabulary

3 The words below are all to do with communication but the letters are in the wrong order. Write the words and use them in the note. Start with the letter shown.

Hi Maya,
When I was working on the computer this morning, I got an **(1)** .... from Roberto in Colombia. He's asked me to post him some photos but I don't have his **(2)** .... there. Could you give it to me, please? I'll be in the library all afternoon, but you can leave a **(3)** .... on my mobile phone. I'm going to write him a long **(4)** .... this evening and put it in the **(5)** .... with the photos.
See you,
Anton

4 Complete the table.

Country	Nationality	Language(s) spoken
China		
Egypt		
Greece		
		Dutch
	Mexican	

Exam skills

5

Reading Part 2

Read the sentences about learning a new language.
Choose the best word (**A**, **B** or **C**) for each space for questions **6–10**.

Example:

0 Bruno .... to learn Polish because his grandmother lives in Poland.
   A wants   **B** believes   **C** enjoys

   Answer: **0** A■ B☐ C☐

---

6 Bruno has .... a six-month Polish course for beginners at the college in town.
   A caught   **B** looked   **C** found

7 He has bought some books and a dictionary, so he is .... to start.
   A easy   **B** ready   **C** busy

8 At the end of the course, he will .... an exam.
   A make   **B** give   **C** take

9 As .... as possible after the exam, he'd like to visit Poland.
   A well   **B** soon   **C** enough

10 He hopes to have an interesting .... with his grandmother there.
   A talk   **B** text   **C** song

20 People

Exam skills

1

Writing Part 7

Complete this email.

Write ONE word for each space for questions **41–50**.

Example: | **0** | from |

> To: Cristina
> From: Rachel
>
> Your postcard **(0)** .... Italy arrived today! It's really strange, **(41)** .... I have some history homework to do on Italy **(42)** .... the moment! Do you mind **(43)** .... I ask you some questions about your famous leader Giuseppe Garibaldi? I have **(44)** .... write about an Italian **(45)** .... was important in the nineteenth century. When **(46)** .... Garibaldi born?
>
> In 1860, he went to Sicily, didn't **(47)** .... ? It's amazing to think that those 1000 soldiers **(48)** .... his won in Palermo – there were many more soldiers on the other side.
>
> Can you tell me **(49)** .... Garibaldi did after 1860? Thanks. I **(50)** .... you'll email me with the answers soon!

Grammar

2   Decide which tense is correct in these sentences.

EXAMPLE:

0 Brooklyn and Romeo (are)/ *have been* the names of David and Victoria Beckham's first two sons.

1 In February 2005, the Beckhams *have had / had* a third son.

2 They *called / were calling* him Cruz.

3 Many people *think / are thinking* that Cruz is a girl's name.

4 The Beckhams *were choosing / chose* this name because they both like the way it *sounds / is sounding*.

5 In a few years' time, Cruz *is going to / will* probably become a popular boy's name in Britain!

3   Re-write these sentences about the American billionaire Donald Trump, correcting any tense errors.

EXAMPLE:

0 Donald Trump is always a very successful businessman.
   Donald Trump has always been a very successful businessman.

1 In January 2005, Trump has got married for the third time.

....

2 Many famous people are seen at the wedding in Florida.

....

3 Trump's new wife Melanie Knauss is coming from Slovenia.

....

4 The French design company Christian Dior makes her wedding dress.

....

Vocabulary

4 Complete the crossword with adjectives. The number of letters is given in brackets.

Across

1 Describes the person or thing you like best. (9)
5 Another word for *sick*. (3)
7 Not married. (6)
9 Something that has never been used is this. (3)
10 You can use this word to describe an attractive woman or girl. (6)
11 If you win lots of competitions, this probably describes you. (5)
15 The opposite of *same*. (9)
17 Not saying anything. (5)
18 The opposite of *wet*. (3)

Down

1 This means being pleasant and open with someone. (8)
2 Another way of saying *sad*. (7)
3 If you need something to drink, this is how you feel. (7)
4 Your best friend is this. (7)
6 The opposite of *high*. (3)
8 Describes a colour that mixes black and white. (4)
12 Describes someone who is helpful to others. (4)
13 The opposite of *interested*. (5)
14 Describes something that makes you laugh. (5)
16 The opposite of *thin*. (3)

Exam skills

5

Writing Part 9

You have agreed to take an Australian tourist called Mike around your town next Saturday. Write an email to Mike.

Say:
- **where** you will meet Mike
- **how long** you can spend with him on Saturday
- **what** you are going to show him.

Write **25–35** words.

Answer key

Unit 1
Grammar

1

Own answers

2

1 Do you see your friend every day?
2 Do you go shopping together?
3 Do you forget to give back your friend's CDs?
4 Have you got your friend's number on speed dial?
5 Do you lend your friend DVDs?
6 Are you often angry with your friend?
7 Can you chat to your friend for hours?
8 Can you tell your friend everything?

3

1 What is your favourite ice cream?
2 When can you meet me at the cinema?
3 How about inviting Laura to your party on Saturday?
4 What have you got for homework tonight? OR What homework have you got for tonight?
5 Why don't you borrow the DVD from Juan?
6 Where does the girl with the long hair come from?

Writing

4

Possible answers
1 She's 13.
2 We go out together on Saturday mornings.
3 We meet in the centre of town.
4 She's got CDs by Beyoncé, Robbie Williams and Mina.
5 Keira Knightley is my favourite film star.

Vocabulary

5

Across: ill   Down: great
        free   pleased
        sad   funny
        true   angry
        bad   good
        boring

u	s	p	e	c	i	a	l	i
i	l	l	r	o	p	n	e	g
n	i	e	l	l	m	g	n	o
t	g	a	t	c	f	r	e	e
a	r	s	c	h	u	y	n	g
l	e	e	s	w	n	e	t	o
s	a	d	e	l	n	g	h	o
a	t	r	u	e	y	b	a	d
k	n	b	o	r	i	n	g	s

6

1 funny
2 true
3 sad
4 ill
5 boring
6 good

Unit 2
Vocabulary

1

Possible answers
Bookshop: book, CD, DVD
Chemist: plasters, shampoo, toothpaste
Newsagent: chocolate, newspaper, sweets

2

2 sofas, tables, chairs
1 shirts, sweaters, belts
G shampoo, make-up, toothpaste
B glasses, plates

3

Across:
- **1** children
- **5** glass
- **6** horse
- **7** apple
- **8** map
- **9** fish
- **11** boxes
- **12** feet

Down:
- **2** half price
- **3** dishes
- **4** newspaper
- **10** toy

¹C	²H	I	L	³D	R	E	⁴N	
	A			I			E	
⁵G	L	A	S	S			W	
	F			⁶H	O	R	S	E
⁷A	P	P	L	E			P	
	R			S		⁸M	A	P
⁹F	I	S	H		¹⁰T		P	
	C			¹¹B	O	X	E	S
¹²F	E	E	T		Y		R	

Grammar

4

1 They've got **some lemons** from Spain.
2 There are **some potatoes**.
3 There aren't **any carrots**.
4 They **haven't (got) any** apples. / They **don't have any** apples.
5 They've got **some** large **tomatoes** but they haven't got **any** small ones.
6 They haven't got **any oranges** left.

5

1 B
2 A
3 C
4 B
5 B
6 C
7 A
8 C

Writing

6

Possible answers

1 My favourite shop is called *Tazz* and you can buy really great clothes there.
2 I go shopping with my friend Lorenzo every Saturday.
3 I'd like to buy the new Jovanotti CD for my friend's birthday.
4 I don't spend much money on sweets or chocolate.
5 The supermarket near us sells cheap T-shirts in different colours.
6 You can buy really cheap books and DVDs on the internet.

Unit 3

Grammar

1

1 I don't like chocolate.
2 My friend doesn't buy apples.
3 Marco makes salad.
4 Anna loves cheese.
5 The cat doesn't drink milk.
6 We don't grow bananas.
7 The cafe sells cola.
8 My father doesn't use a cookbook.
9 My grandmother cooks our dinner.
10 Tessa and Piero don't come home for lunch.

2

1 We always have dinner at six thirty.
2 The food festival is usually in August.
3 Mauro often has a cake on his birthday.
4 My brother is never late for meals!
5 Do you usually drink coffee in the afternoon?
6 Correct. Also possible: I sometimes buy a sandwich for lunch. / I buy a sandwich for lunch sometimes.
7 I always shop at the supermarket.
8 My mother often invites my friends to dinner.

3

1 It's two forty-five; it's a quarter to three.
2 It's five thirty; it's half past five.
3 It's six minutes past three.
4 It's eleven fifty; it's ten to twelve.
5 It's eight twenty; it's twenty minutes past eight.
6 It's nine fifty-five; it's five to ten.

Vocabulary

4

1 carrot
2 lemon
3 potato
4 apple
5 tomato
6 banana
7 grape

Writing

5

Possible answers

1 My birthday is on 29th December.
2 On my birthday I always have a big party.
3 I never go to school on my birthday.
4 At my party I play a lot of games and dance with my friends.
5 My friends sometimes give me wonderful presents.

Exam skills

6

1 H
2 G
3 C
4 D
5 E

Unit 4
Grammar

1

1 took
2 wanted
3 didn't start / did not start
4 were
5 went
6 crossed
7 travelled
8 were
9 decided
10 didn't stop / did not stop
11 didn't have / did not have
12 wasn't / was not
13 arrived
14 died
15 got
16 took

2

1 How did he travel? He travelled by ship.
2 How many ships did he take? He took five ships.
3 Where did he lose a ship? He lost a ship near South America.
4 How much food and water did they have? They didn't have much food or water.
5 Where did Magellan die? Magellan died in the Philippines.
6 Which ship got home safely? The *Victoria* got home safely.
7 How long did it take the *Victoria* to travel around the world? It took two years and 353 days.

3

1 caught
2 chose
3 drank
4 flew
5 grew
6 made
7 met
8 paid
9 said
10 spoke
11 stood
12 thought
13 wore
14 wrote
15 did

Exam skills

4

36 coach
37 horse
38 boat
39 plane
40 bicycles

Writing

5

A

Dear Gianni
Last week I went to Thailand. I stayed in a big hotel near the beach. I went swimming and played tennis every day.
from

B

Dear Emilio
I went to see my cousin Sandro in New York. My friend Jo came with me and we had a great time. We went by plane from Heathrow airport.
from

Unit 5
Vocabulary

1

1 cats
2 dolphins
3 lions
4 horse
5 elephants
6 fish
7 bears
8 monkey
9 spiders
10 dog

2

1 make
2 did
3 took
4 took/did
5 made
6 did you spend
7 did
8 made
9 spent
10 made

Grammar

3

1 A
2 A
3 C
4 A
5 B
6 A
7 C
8 C
9 A

4

1 Goldfish are easy to look after **and** they cost less to buy than a cat or a dog.
2 Goldfish can live in a glass bowl **but** it is important to change the water every week.
3 You can put different things in your goldfish bowl, like a small castle, **and/or** you can grow plants in it.
4 Give your goldfish food two to three times a day **but** give it only a small amount.
5 You can go on holiday **but** don't forget to ask a friend to look after your goldfish.

Writing

5

Elisa
You can go to the zoo in our town to see **bears**, penguins **and elephants**. It is open every weekend **and** we can go **together**. We can **travel** by bus **or** go by car, if you want. I like the penguins best **because** they swim so **well** underwater.
See you **soon**.

Unit 6
Vocabulary

1

1 tennis, beautiful
2 uncle, aunt, dinner
3 telephone, tomorrow
4 apartment, second
5 friends, cinema
6 interesting
7 easier
8 bigger, better

2

1 train 2 apple 3 book 4 letter 5 eye 6 truck
7 elephant 8 newspaper 9 nose 10 ice cream
11 shoe

1	2	3	4	5	6	7	8	9	10	11
t	a	b	l	e		t	e	n	n	i	s

The sport is table tennis.

3

1 Hi, is that Claudia?
2 No, it's Amanda. Claudia isn't in.
3 Hi, Amanda, it's Cecilia here.
4 Oh, hi, Cecilia. Claudia's at the beach.
5 Could you ask her to ring me this evening?
6 Sure, no problem.
7 Great. See you soon, I hope.
8 Yes, I'll be at the party this weekend.
9 OK, see you then. Bye.

Grammar

4

1 the best
2 farther/further
3 the cheapest
4 younger
5 more expensive
6 (much) better
7 earlier
8 warmer
9 the most popular
10 latest

Exam skills

5

6 B
7 A
8 C
9 A
10 A

Writing

6

Dear Flavio,
Last weekend **I** went to the city centre. **I** went skateboarding with my best friend **Luca**. We had a great time there.
Love, **Pietro**

Unit 7
Exam skills

1

28 C
29 C
30 B
31 A
32 C
33 B
34 B
35 A

Grammar

2

1 b was trying on
2 a was wearing **b** became **c** threw **d** made
3 a was chatting **b** ran **c** stopped **d** asked
e were looking

3

Possible answers

1 I was wearing a blue T-shirt and jeans.
2 I was studying five subjects – science, Italian, maths, history and French.
3 I'm staying in and doing my homework.
4 Lazio and Inter were playing, but I'm not sure which other teams were.
5 My uncle is coming to stay with me soon.

Vocabulary

4

Across: wool Down: size
belt jacket
hat sweater
shorts cotton
trainers shoe
button shirt
  trousers

s	j	a	s	o	c	k	s	t
i	a	l	w	o	o	l	h	r
z	c	b	e	l	t	g	i	o
e	k	h	a	t	t	r	r	u
e	e	x	t	h	o	s	t	s
s	t	e	e	w	n	h	w	e
s	h	o	r	t	s	o	h	r
a	t	r	a	i	n	e	r	s
r	t	b	u	t	t	o	n	r

Writing

5

1 trousers
2 shoe
3 size
4 shirt
5 cotton
6 jacket
7 button
8 hat
9 *Possible answer*
there are flowers and a bird on it. There's a banana too!

Unit 8
Exam skills

1

1 E
2 G
3 F
4 A
5 H

Grammar

2

1 You can come here by train.
2 I can come on Monday or Friday.
3 Last night I had to do my homework.
4 You can go to the IMAX cinema.
5 Correct.
6 I work in the week but you could come at the weekend.
7 You can feed the fish at Mangabeiras Park.
8 I was at the back so I couldn't see anything.

3

1 must
2 can't
3 may
4 can't
5 may
6 must

Vocabulary

4

1 guitar
2 speakers
3 dance
4 piano
5 drums
6 singer

Exam skills

5

41 like/love/enjoy
42 to
43 It/This
44 ago
45 one/something
46 was/happened
47 There
48 each/every
49 Why
50 can/could

Unit 9

Grammar

1

1 see
2 best
3 am going to
4 In
5 lots of
6 anywhere
7 spend
8 who
9 go

2

1 e
2 d
3 g
4 f
5 h
6 b
7 c
8 a

3

Possible answers

1 I think I will make a lot of money.
2 I don't think I will have any children.
3 I think I will be a journalist.
4 I think I will live in a big house.
5 I think I will have lots of holidays.
6 I think I will drive a Porsche.
7 I think I will be very happy.

Vocabulary

4

Across: book
space
cruise
Australia

Down: Earth
fly
souvenirs
travel
Switzerland

e	a	s	j	o	u	r	n	e	y	y	s
a	u	s	i	e	a	a	s	w	r	h	w
r	w	o	r	r	b	o	o	k	d	n	i
t	c	u	t	u	s	i	i	r	l	k	t
h	c	v	r	s	p	a	c	e	m	n	z
o	f	e	a	f	t	k	u	q	c	x	e
l	l	n	v	b	y	l	e	u	a	s	r
h	y	i	e	x	c	r	u	i	s	e	l
y	v	r	l	c	i	f	r	y	g	z	a
w	d	s	t	n	f	c	s	f	m	w	n
a	g	a	u	s	t	r	a	l	i	a	d
q	h	s	k	b	d	v	b	d	t	k	h

Exam skills

5

36 camping
37 brochure
38 hotel
39 tourists
40 museum

Unit 10

Exam skills

1

21 A
22 C
23 B
24 C
25 A
26 B
27 B

Vocabulary

2

1	**2**	**3**	
r	e	d	+

4	**5**	**6**	**7**	
b	l	u	e	=

p	u	r	p	l	e

Grammar

3

1 The bed wasn't made.
2 The room wasn't cleaned.
3 The clothes weren't put in the wardrobe.
4 The cups and plates weren't washed.
5 The TV wasn't turned off.
6 The wardrobe door wasn't closed.
7 The light wasn't turned off.

4

1 were painted
2 is visited
3 was made
4 was given
5 is used
6 is kept
7 was designed

Unit 11

Vocabulary

1

b surfing **c** table tennis **d** skiing **e** volleyball

2

1 surfing
2 skiing
3 swimming
4 volleyball
5 skiing
6 swimming
7 volleyball
8 skiing
9 table tennis

3

1 board
2 poles
3 kick
4 net
5 boots
6 club
7 team
8 gloves
9 table

The sport in the grey box is basketball.

Grammar

4

1 How are you getting to Saturday's competition?
2 Which country/team does Christian Ronaldo play football for?
3 Who does Gianni play tennis with?
4 When does the gym close? OR When does the gym stay open until? OR When is the gym open (until)?
5 Why did the referee stop the match?
6 How many people were (there) in the stadium?
7 Where are you going to go sailing? OR Where are you going sailing?

5

1 keeping
2 cycling
3 driving
4 sitting
5 running
6 climbing
7 exercising
8 dancing

Exam skills

6

11 B
12 A
13 B
14 C
15 A

Unit 12

Vocabulary

1

1 brother
2 uncle
3 grandmother
4 aunt
5 daughter
6 sister

Grammar

2

1 Our
2 Your mine
3 her
4 theirs
5 my
6 yours

Writing

3

Sentences 2, 3 and 5 answer the questions in postcard A; sentences 1 and 4 answer the questions in postcard B.

4

Sample answers

A

Hi Ernesto!
Thanks for your postcard. Everyone was there for Uncle Charles's birthday, including his brother from Australia. He really loved having us all together and he never stopped smiling! There was a lovely cake with 60 candles on it.
Love, Juliette

B

Dear Yasmin,
Thanks for your postcard. Two weeks ago, my aunt invited us to her house in the country. We were all there to see my cousin's new baby. I had a really great time!
Yours, Juliette

Exam skills

5

28 B

29 C

30 A

31 B

32 C

33 B

34 C

35 A

Unit 13
Exam skills

1

41 ago

42 and

43 to

44 were/had

45 at

46 lot

47 When

48 had/took

49 spent/enjoyed

50 Did

Grammar

2

Possible answers

 1 Athens is sunnier/hotter than Rome. OR Rome isn't as sunny/hot as Athens.
 2 Russia is bigger than Canada. OR Canada isn't as big as Russia.
 3 The river Nile is longer than the river Amazon. OR The river Amazon isn't as long as the river Nile.
 4 The Empire State Building is higher/taller than the Eiffel Tower. OR The Eiffel Tower is not as high/tall as the Empire State Building.
 5 Today is as cold as yesterday.
 6 June is sunnier than October. OR October isn't as sunny as June.
 7 The amount of rain is/was the same in December as in January.
 8 New Zealand is warmer than Antarctica.
 9 Venice is further north than Rome.
10 Mount Everest is higher than Mount Kilimanjaro. OR Mount Kilimanjaro isn't as high as Mount Everest.

3

 1 difficult

 2 ill

 3 thin

 4 busy

 5 young

 6 hot

 7 noisy

 8 clean

 9 small

10 old

Vocabulary

4

thunderstormsnowindry

5

 1 hot

 2 warm

 3 sunny

 4 rain

 5 windy

 6 cold

The word in the grey box is tornado.

Writing

6

Possible answer

Hi!/Hi

In July, the weather is quite good in my country. It doesn't rain very much so you don't need an umbrella or a raincoat. It's better to bring T-shirts and a swimming costume when you come to visit me. Don't forget a towel!!/.

Unit 14

Vocabulary

1

word
dictionary
sentence
page
email
envelope
homework
journalist
message
note

2

Across: history
         music

Down: science
       sport
       geography
       maths
       art

l	a	n	g	u	a	g	e	s	a	l
j	g	e	s	e	y	e	g	m	s	v
k	n	e	p	c	v	o	u	a	h	m
r	z	u	o	a	t	g	f	t	s	n
s	s	w	r	g	v	r	n	h	m	h
c	a	c	t	y	r	a	t	s	h	a
i	w	w	d	t	f	p	g	h	j	r
e	s	f	g	c	m	h	p	x	b	t
n	j	e	f	j	l	y	i	h	y	h
c	d	t	h	i	s	t	o	r	y	b
e	l	m	u	s	i	c	e	u	c	f

Exam skills

3

6 C
7 B
8 A
9 B
10 C

Grammar

4

1 a nice new comic
2 the boring old history book
3 a lovely little bookshop
4 the expensive American magazine
5 a famous young French writer
6 a large modern university library
7 the dirty old bookshelves
8 the friendly young English teacher
9 a lovely little yellow table
10 the excellent Japanese computers

5

Possible answers

1 I prefer to read science fiction books rather than detective books.
2 I prefer to study history rather than English.
3 I prefer to watch TV rather than study.
4 I prefer to go to the beach rather than a swimming pool.
5 I prefer to play computer games rather than play the piano.

Writing

6

Dear Elena,
Do you like reading? I do and **too** of my friends like it **two**. But sometimes **their to** many **thinks** to do and I don't have time **too** read. Do you **by** a lot of books? I don't.
I use the library.
When I leave school I don't know **weather** I **won't too** teach or write books. What about you?
Buy for now!
Love,
Marisa

1 too
2 there are
3 too
4 things
5 to
6 buy
7 whether
8 want
9 to
10 Bye

Unit 15
Vocabulary

1
actor
bodyguard
chef
doctor
engineer
farmer
gardener
hairdresser
instructor
journalist
king
lifeguard
mechanic
nurse
officer
photographer
queen
receptionist
shop assistant
tour guide
undercover agent
van driver
waiter
xylophone player
yoga teacher
zookeeper

Grammar

2
1 Jan has been the band's manager since February.
2 Three years ago, Helen became a pilot.
3 Our class visited an artist's studio yesterday.
4 The Queen gave Ellen MacArthur a special award in 2005 after her round-the-world race.
5 Ben has never studied chemistry before.

Exam skills

3
16 E
17 C
18 G
19 A
20 D

Unit 16
Vocabulary

1
Across: helicopter
passenger
take off
go
bicycle
park
fly
boat
board
ticket
Down: trip
airport
book
flight
get off
coach

2

1 board
2 coach
3 airport
4 trip
5 park
6 ticket
7 get off

Grammar

3

1 should
2 can't
3 must
4 mustn't
5 need
6 may
7 don't have to
8 could

Writing

4

Dear Roz and Tim,
Here are some **direktions** to our house for next weekend. When you **live** the motorway, turn right at the **rundabout** – it'll say **univirsity** and city centre. Keep on that road for about two kilometres **untill** you come to a big petrol station **whit** a blue and yellow sign. Turn right **their** and go over the bridge. Just after you've crossed the river, you'll see the **hospetal** on your left. Take the second turning on the left after that – it's called **Musium** Street. We're at **nummer** 54.
See you on Saturday,
Love,
Sharon and Eduardo

1 leave
2 roundabout
3 university
4 until
5 with
6 there
7 hospital
8 Museum
9 number

Exam skills

5

51 Madrid
52 (Tuesday) 16 April or 16/04
53 Heathrow
54 05.40
55 £44.99

Unit 17

Exam skills

1

28 B
29 B
30 A
31 C
32 A
33 A
34 B
35 C

Grammar

2

Possible/own answers

1 I phone my friends to have a chat about football.
2 I listen to music to relax.
3 I work hard at school to get good marks.
4 I buy new clothes to look fashionable.
5 I use a computer to send emails.

3

1 Take the bus to get to the town centre.
2 The best way to get back from the cinema is to take a taxi.
3 Go to classes to learn computing.
4 We can go to buy a new computer in the mall.
5 I am really happy you will come to visit me.
6 It is better for you not to play computer games.
7 It's a great place to take vacations.
8 I want to get a new mobile.
9 You must see that new film.
10 They decided to buy a pink iPod mini.

Vocabulary

4

1 watched/saw
2 take
3 make
4 taking/doing
5 get
6 do
7 make
8 makes
9 see
10 see/watch

5

1 chat room
2 technology
3 internet
4 video
5 gadgets
6 robot
7 laptop
8 text message

Writing

6

Sample answer

Dear Rosa

My parents gave me a new computer game called 'The Sims' for my birthday. I really like it because it's fun and you can build houses and give the people jobs. It's great.

Love

Tania

Unit 18
Exam skills

1

21 C
22 A
23 A
24 B
25 C
26 B
27 A

Vocabulary

2

Possible answers

1 back – not on your arm
2 police officer – not a job to do with health
3 hospital – not a vehicle
4 a diet – not an illness
5 neck – you only have one of them

Grammar

3

1 Last night I had a sore throat. OR I had a sore throat last night.
2 Two weeks ago I stayed in a very famous hospital. OR I stayed in a very famous hospital two weeks ago.
3 I very much like my doctor. OR I like my doctor very much.
4 In the night I was sick. OR I was sick in the night.
5 My new diet is amazing.
6 Today I need to go to the chemist's. OR I need to go to the chemist's today.
7 Why don't you take an aspirin?
8 This afternoon I felt terrible so I went home. OR I felt terrible this afternoon so I went home. OR I felt so terrible this afternoon, I went home.

4

1 sleep, will/'ll feel
2 go, will not / won't get
3 eat, will/'ll live
4 do not / don't eat, will/'ll stay
5 will/'ll earn, become
6 will/'ll you do, get

Writing

5

Sample answer
Dear Mikey,
Last night I had a dream about flying. I was flying through the air above the school. When I woke up I felt very happy.
Tomo

Unit 19
Grammar

1

1 with at/in
2 on at
3 in on
4 in at
5 of in
6 correct
7 at in
8 on at/in
9 to at/in
10 at in
11 to in
12 in at
13 on at

2

1 on
2 in
3 By/At
4 In/During
5 On
6 In
7 On
8 At

Vocabulary

3

1 email
2 address
3 message
4 letter
5 envelope

4

Possible answers

Country	Nationality	Language(s) spoken
China	Chinese	Chinese
Egypt	Egyptian	Arabic
Greece	Greek	Greek
Holland	Dutch	Dutch
Mexico	Mexican	Spanish

Exam skills

5

- **6** C
- **7** B
- **8** C
- **9** B
- **10** A

Unit 20
Exam skills

1

- **41** because/as/since
- **42** at
- **43** if
- **44** to
- **45** who/that
- **46** was
- **47** he
- **48** of
- **49** what
- **50** hope

Grammar

2

- **1** had
- **2** called
- **3** think
- **4** chose sounds
- **5** will

3

1. In January 2005, Trump got married for the third time.
2. Many famous people were seen at the wedding in Florida.
3. Trump's new wife Melanie Knauss comes from Slovenia.
4. The French design company Christian Dior made her wedding dress.

Vocabulary

4

1 F	A	V	O	2 U	R	I	3 T	E			4 S
R				N			H				P
5 I	L	6 L		H		7 S	I	N	8 G	L	E
E		O		A			R		R		C
9 N	E	W		P			S		E		I
D				10 P	R	E	T	T	Y		A
11 L	U	C	12 K	Y			Y				L
Y			I					13 B		14 F	
			N					O		U	
			15 D	I	16 F	F	E	R	E	N	T
					A			E		N	
17 Q	U	I	E	T	T			18 D	R	Y	

Exam skills

5

Sample answer

Hi Mike!

I'll meet you under the station clock next
Saturday. I'm free until about 5 p.m., so we'll have
plenty of time together. We can see the castle, and
have lunch there.

See you,

Tomasz

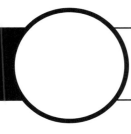

Acknowledgements

The authors would like to thank Sue Ashcroft at Cambridge University Press for her constant diligence and support and Stephanie White at Kamae for her creative design solutions.

The authors and publishers are grateful to the authors, publishers and others who have given permission for the use of copyright material identified in the text. It has not been possible to identify the sources of all the material used and in such cases the publishers would welcome information from copyright owners. Apologies are expressed for any omissions.

Text on p.22 adapted from a text by Gabriel from 'I live in a castle' from CBBC Newsround at http://news.bbc.co.uk/cbbcnews/hi/newsid_4050000/ newsid_4059000/4059057.stm; text on p.27 adapted from a text from BBC News at bbcnews.com at http://news.bbc.co.uk/1/hi/world/europe/3685952.stm.

The publishers are grateful to the following for permission to reproduce copyright photographs and material:

Key: tr = top right, bc = bottom centre, tl = top left, br = bottom right, bl = bottom left.

Alamy pp 10 (Stock Montage, Inc.), 15 (SuperStock), 19 (Photofusion Picture Library), 22 (The National Trust Photolibrary), 24tr (Buzz Pictures); Corbis pp 13 (Tim Davis), 20 (David Muench), 24bc, 24tl (LWA-Dann Tardif), 33 (Stephen Hird/Reuters), 40 (Bettmann); Getty Images pp 16 (Ryan Pierse), 24br (Arthur Tilley), 28 (Greg Ceo), 42 (Hulton Archive); Kobal Collection p 36 (Lucas Film/ 20th Century Fox); Charlotta Smeds p 27; Punchstock p 24bl (BananaStock).

Illustrations by:
Tim Davies pp 6, 7, 14b, 23b, 30; Kamae Design pp 8, 10, 29, 40; Gillian Martin pp 9, 13, 14t, 17, 23t, 25, 34, 38, 39; Colin Meir p 32.

Picture research by Pictureresearch.co.uk